THE SECRETS OF THE DOLPHINS

What are dolphins, and where did they come from?

THE SECRETS OF THE DOLPHINS

by Diana Reiss

Illustrated by Laurie O'Keefe

A Byron Preiss Book

AN AVON CAMELOT BOOK

To Morgan, to the future. —D.R.

THE SECRETS OF THE DOLPHINS is an original publication of Avon Books. This work has never before appeared in book form.

AVON BOOKS
A division of
The Hearst Corporation
105 Madison Avenue
New York, New York 10016

Special thanks to Ellen Krieger, our editor at Avon Books

Editor: Gillian Bucky
Assistant Editor: Kathy Huck
Book design by Michael Goode
Cover design by Stephen Brenninkmeyer
Front cover photograph copyright © Diana Reiss

Library of Congress Cataloging in Publication Data:
Reiss, Diana.
    The secrets of the dolphins / Diana Reiss.
        p. cm.—(Camelot World) (An Avon Camelot book)
    "A Byron Preiss Book "
    Includes index.
    Summary: Introduces the world of dolphins, their physical characteristics, behavior, and interaction with humans.
1. Dolphins—Juvenile literature. [1. Dolphins.] I. Title. II. Series.
QL737. C432R46   1991   91-7678
599.5'3—dc20   AC

First Avon Camelot Printing: May 1991

"Camelot World" is a trademark of Byron Preiss Visual Publications, Inc.

CAMELOT TRADEMARK REG. U.S. PAT. OFF. AND IN OTHER COUNTRIES, MARCA REGISTRADA, HECHO EN U.S.A.

Printed in the U.S.A.
OPM 10 9 8 7 6 5 4 3 2 1

CONTENTS

Dolphins live in a watery world.

INTRODUCTION

I remember the first time I saw dolphins in the wild. One afternoon I was walking on a beach in Cape May, New Jersey, when I saw the surface of the sea break with the graceful bodies of five sleek gray dolphins. They were heading south, swimming in a tight formation along the coastline. Rocky jetties stretched out, like arms, to the dolphins that swam just beyond their reach. I ran out on one of the jetties to get a closer look. They were just a few feet away from me! One of the dolphins was very young and was playing in the waves, quickly returning to its mother when it got too far away. The older dolphins began diving down around the edges of the jetty. It looked as if they might be searching for fish along the rocky barrier.

As I watched them leaping in the waves, I found myself imagining what it would be like to live in such a world. Suddenly, I felt as though I were out there with them, now one of them, looking back at the shoreline at all the strange, two-legged creatures dotting the beach. But just as quickly I was back on the jetty again, a human being once more. I wished that I could jump in the ocean and swim along with them. I longed to learn more about their secret world, the world of the dolphin.

For thousands of years, people have been fascinated by dolphins. Whether in the wild or in captivity, these remarkable animals have captured the interest and imagination of scientists and others who have watched them and played with them. There are ancient paintings showing dolphins rescuing drowning people. Other paintings show children riding on dolphins. Many old and new stories tell about how dolphins saved drowning people or came to shore seeking out humans for play. Other stories tell of dolphins cooperating with fishermen to herd schools of fish for capture.

Are these stories real? What do we really

People have always been fascinated by dolphins.

know about the dolphin? What *are* dolphins, anyway, and where did they come from? What is their world like? How do they live and survive in a water environment? Do they communicate with each other? How intelligent are they?

These were the animals I had chosen to study. Even before I saw them frolicking in the ocean, I was intrigued with dolphins because of their apparent intelligence and social nature. After obtaining a Ph.D. in speech and communication science, I started a dolphin-research project called Project Circe (pro-nounced sur-cee) at an oceanarium and wild animal facility called Marine World Africa USA in Vallejo, California. An oceanarium is an aquarium for marine mammals such as whales, dolphins, porpoises, sea otters, seals, sea lions, and walruses. For the past nine years I have had the wonderful opportunity to observe and learn from a group of bottlenose dolphins that live at Marine World. The group is composed of two females, Terry and Circe, and their male offspring, Pan and Delphi. I observed Pan and Delphi being born and watched and recorded how they learned to communicate with one another. I saw them cooperate with each other to accomplish different tasks. Above all, I began to learn how to let these remarkable mammals show us what they are capable of doing rather than us trying to get them to do things we want them to do.

In this book I will introduce you to some of what we know about the world of the dolphin. The more you know about dolphins the better you can appreciate and respect them.

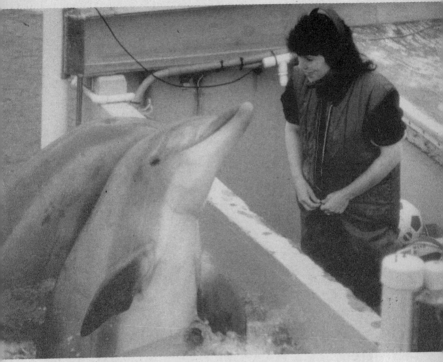

The author with the dolphins of Project Circe.

Dolphins and humans have been friends for a long time.

CHAPTER ONE

Dolphins and Humans

Throughout history there have been many stories and myths about the relationship between humans and dolphins. An ancient Greek myth tells how the god Apollo became a dolphin and led Greek sailors to Delphi, the new center of the ancient world. Greek sailors believed that dolphins were lucky omens, and that if they were lost the dolphins would lead them safely back to shore. There are also many tales about dolphins saving drowning people by carrying them back to shore. One of the most famous stories of all is that of Arion, a famous poet and musician. According to legends, dolphins saved Arion from drowning at sea after he jumped overboard from a ship to avoid being killed by the crew. Paintings and coins from long ago show

Arion and other people riding on the backs of dolphins.

Some of these old tales may just be myths, but many of them may have been based on real events that were exaggerated over the ages, like any good story. Even today, people tell of similar experiences with dolphins. There are reports in our newspapers about dolphins saving sailors and swimmers. People claim to have been saved from drowning by dolphins who appeared suddenly and carried them safely back to shore. Sailors also tell about how dolphins led their ships safely through dangerous waters. For more than 20 years, beginning in 1888, a Risso's dolphin (a species of dolphin that swims in warm and tropical waters) named Pelorus Jack accompanied ships crossing Cook's Strait, New Zealand. Pelorus Jack would ride the bow waves around the front of ships as they ploughed through the water. He became well known to the sailors and passengers.

Many ancient and modern accounts tell of friendly dolphins playing with people. Long ago, Aristotle wrote about dolphins and young boys playing together and forming strong friendships. Similar relationships between dolphins and children are found today. A well-known instance of this took place in a small town, Opononi, in New Zealand, that has a bay into which dolphins swim from the sea. One dolphin, called Opo, would swim close to shore and play with young children, and with one little girl in particular named Jill. Another friendly dolphin, Donald, played with divers for years off the coast of England. And on the

coast of Australia there is a beach called Monkey Mia, where dolphins swim into shallow waters and play with children and adults. People play with and feed the dolphins there, and year after year the dolphins return. Mother dolphins bring their calves (baby dolphins), and this practice is passed on from generation to generation.

Two thousand years ago, Roman poets wrote of dolphins herding fish into the nets of fishermen. Today, on the coasts of Africa and

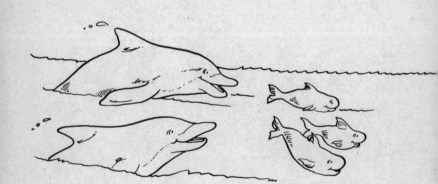

South America, there are villages in which fishermen and dolphins work together in cooperative fishing. Dolphins herd fish into long nets that the fishermen hold outstretched in shallow waters along the beaches. Both the fishermen and the dolphins get fish this way.

So it seems that humans and dolphins have had a relationship for thousands of years. Many of these old tales may be true, although they have been embellished over time by our imagination and fancy.

Saving a Lost Humpback Whale

With all the accounts of dolphins saving people, it is nice to know that we try to save them, too. This story shows how much people care about marine mammals and that we can help to protect them.

On October 10, 1985, a 40-ton, 40-foot-long humpback whale strayed from his ocean habitat, the deep waters of the Pacific Ocean, and wandered into San Francisco Bay. Humpback whales are members of an endangered species, and they live in the North Pacific, North Atlantic, and in southern oceans. For three weeks, this whale, named Humphrey, continued to journey 80 miles inland. First, Humphrey set off up the Sacramento River, which runs into the bay. From there he swam into the narrow and often shallow sloughs or river deltas that branched out from the river. His inland journey sparked worldwide concern for the fate of this lost whale. Would he survive? Would he find his way back to the ocean?

In a joint effort, the California Marine Mammal Center, government agencies, scientists, politicians, and private citizens cooperated in a massive effort to save this confused whale.

Throngs of people gathered on the river banks to catch a glimpse of the whale as the rescue team tried to herd Humphrey back out to sea. First, the team formed a semicircle of boats behind Humphrey and banged on long iron pipes hung over the sides of the boats. The pipes were capped and filled with water to create low, chiming underwater sounds.They used the boats and underwater sounds as a barrier to move Humphrey in the right direction, back to the sea. This worked only in the very shallow and narrow deltas. The rescue team then played recordings of humpback whale sounds to Humphrey from a small boat, and he followed the boat back out to sea! The crowds cheered as they watched Humphrey swim under the Golden Gate Bridge and back home into the Pacific Ocean.

CHAPTER TWO

What Are Dolphins?

Dolphins are mammals that live totally in the water. These marine mammals are part of a larger group, or order, called *Cetacea*, which includes all whales and porpoises as well as dolphins. Dolphins are actually small-toothed whales of the family *Delphinidae*.

Many people think that dolphins and porpoises are the same animal. They do look similar, but there are important differences. The head of the dolphin is different from that of the porpoise. Dolphins have a very distinctive beak called the *rostrum*, and porpoises do not. The dolphin's rostrum looks like a nose, but it is not, as we shall see later. Dolphin teeth are cone shaped, while porpoise teeth are more triangular or spade shaped, and dolphins have curved dorsal fins (the fins

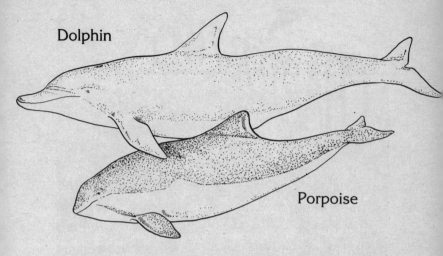

Dolphin

Porpoise

on their backs), while most porpoises have tri-angular dorsal fins.

When most people think of dolphins, they think of the bottlenose dolphin (*Tursiops truncatus*) that is seen in most oceanaria. But there are actually about 30 different species of dolphin living in the oceans, bays, and some rivers of the world. They live in both warm and cold waters.

Most dolphins are gray or black on their upper body (dorsal region) and a lighter shade of gray or white on their belly (ventral region). This two-tone coloration acts as a camouflage

Looking at Dorsal Fins

People often wonder how we tell dolphins apart from one another. There are several ways. Many dolphins have distinctly different dorsal fins. Some fins are curved or shaped in a particular way. Some have nicks or shark bites, and others lean to one side or the other. Scientists who study dolphins in the wild take photographs of the individuals and look at their dorsal fins to identify particular dolphins. This technique is called *photoidentification.* Anyone can learn to do this with a little practice.

that protects them from their enemies, such as sharks or killer whales. Seen from below, dolphins are light and blend in against the water illuminated from above. From above, they appear darker and thus blend in with the water around them and the ocean floor.

Scientists who study dolphins in an oceanarium quickly learn to see the more subtle differences between individuals. Dolphins' faces look really different once you become familiar with them. For example, Terry has smaller, more almond-shaped eyes, while Circe has larger, round eyes. Dolphins are often different shades of gray. Terry is a much darker shade of gray than is Circe. All these more subtle characteristics make it easy to tell them apart.

Bottlenose dolphins can also vary greatly in size. They generally are six to nine feet long, but some bottlenose dolphins living off the coast of Great Britain grow to 13 feet. Dolphins weigh between 250 and 900 pounds and have one of the largest and most complex and well-developed brains of any animal. It weighs about 1,600 grams and is similar in

The crowd may not be able to tell these dolphins apart, but the dolphin trainers, who work with the animals daily, have learned to recognize the individuals as easily as you recognize your own friends.

size to the human brain (1,350 grams).

The dolphin breathes air through its blowhole, two openings that are its nostrils on the top of its head. The blowhole leads directly to the lungs. Like other mammals, the dolphin has a backbone and gives birth to live babies. Dolphin calves nurse, getting milk from their mothers.

All mammals have hair. What about the dolphin? Adult dolphins are hairless, but infant dolphins are born with little hairs called *vibrissae* on their beaks. These hairs fall out a few days after birth. Dolphins' skin is very soft, smooth, and sensitive to the touch. Some people think that it feels like the surface of a hard-boiled egg or the inner tube of a tire. Dolphins spend a lot of time rubbing and caressing each other. Most dolphins who live in oceanaria seem to enjoy getting rubbed or tickled by humans as well.

Dolphins can live to be 50 or 60 years old. Scientists can determine the age of a dolphin similarly to how we figure out the age of a tree. To find out how old a tree is, we cut through the trunk horizontally and count the

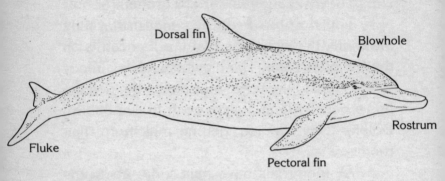

Dorsal fin

Blowhole

Rostrum

Fluke

Pectoral fin

number of rings it has. To figure out a dolphin's age, scientists will pull a tooth from the dolphin's jaw and cut it in half lengthwise. Like tree trunks, dolphins' teeth have rings made from layers of enamel that get deposited every year. Soaking the tooth in an acid solution makes those rings visible. By counting the number of rings, scientists can tell the age of the dolphin.

Dolphins' Ancestors

Scientists think that dolphins evolved from land mammals over the course of millions of years. Fossils found of the teeth, skull, and skeletons of the earliest cetaceans suggest that they may have been early carnivores, or meat eaters. Certain aspects of dolphin behavior and anatomy suggest that they may have had a common ancestor with omnivorous (plant- and meat-eating) ungulates. Members of the ungulate family today include deer, goats, sheep, antelope, and many other grazing and herd animals. The dolphins' land ancestors had four legs and a tail and breathed air through nostrils on the front of their snouts. They probably lived at the water's edge, finding their food both on land and in the water.

About 60 million years ago, the dolphins' ancestors made a gradual change from living on the land to living completely in the water. In order to accomplish this, many changes had to occur in their bodies. For example, their bodies became very streamlined so they could glide through the water with great speed and little resistance. Their front legs became flippers. These flippers, called pectoral fins, are shaped like paddles and help the dolphin steer and maneuver in the water. The bones inside the pectoral fins look a lot like the bones in our hands. The rear legs of dolphins' ancestors gradually disappeared. Their tails evolved into large, flat horizontal fins called flukes, which dolphins move up and down to propel themselves through the water. Their powerful flukes have made dolphins one of the fastest swimmers in the sea. They can swim up to 25 miles per hour (40 kph).

It was also important for dolphins to be able to breathe while living in the water. Over millions of years, this problem has been solved in a very unusual way. By a gradual process of evolution, the dolphins' nostrils moved from the front of their heads, where they are in most mammals, to the *top* of their heads. These "nostrils" are called the blowhole. Dolphins developed the ability to close their blowhole tightly so that water cannot get in, and to open it when they need to breathe.

The development of the blowhole has made it easier for dolphins to breath while lying on the water surface or coming up for air. Unlike humans', dolphins' breathing is under voluntary control. This means dolphins have to decide when to take a breath, and in between breaths the blowhole remains tightly closed so that water cannot get in. Dolphins can breathe only when they come to the water surface; otherwise, they would inhale water and die. This is another important adaptation to a marine life. Dolphins can stay underwater for up to six minutes, but they usually take more frequent breaths, two or three times a minute.

What Happens to Dolphins Underwater?

How deep do you think dolphins can dive? Scientists in the navy trained one dolphin named Tuffy to dive to 1,000 feet in the ocean. Tuffy was also trained to trigger a camera and take a picture of himself at that depth. The photograph showed that at that depth, the increased water pressure collapsed his rib cage and lungs. This didn't hurt Tuffy a bit. Dolphins have a free-floating rib cage that can collapse and let them dive to great depths. This is another special adaptation of their bodies to a marine life.

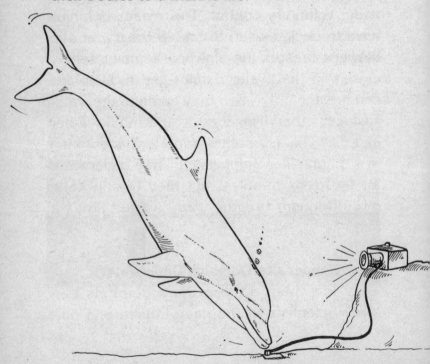

How Do Dolphins Sleep?

All mammals need to sleep. How do dolphins sleep if they always have to decide when to breathe? The answer is that dolphins never go to sleep completely. The dolphin brain is divided into two parts, called hemispheres, one on the right and one on the left. Scientists have discovered that only one hemisphere sleeps at a time, while the other stays awake to control breathing and swimming. When dolphins sleep they either lie motionless at the water surface, or swim at a slower rate, sometimes with one eye closed.

A dolphin sleeps with one eye closed.

The Senses of the Dolphin

Unlike most mammals, dolphins have no sense of smell. This sense was lost in their adaptation to a marine life. But they do have a sense of taste, and they often swim with their mouths open and tongues sticking out. They also have excellent vision in water and in air. In oceanaria, they can rise several feet above the water surface and touch objects that are suspended above their pools. We think they may also have some color vision. Dolphins can even see through the water surface, from underwater into air. For example, from underwater they can follow people walking around their pools and see hand signals their trainers give them. Our eyes are not adapted for this kind of vision. When you are underwater in a swimming pool you cannot see through the water surface into the air.

Dolphins also have excellent hearing. A large part of their brain is involved in processing sound and listening to what is going on in their environment. They no longer have external ears to catch sound as we and so many other land animals have. The species lost these gradually as their bodies became more streamlined for the aquatic environment. All that you can see of their outer ears are small pinhole-sized openings several inches behind their eyes. The internal ear and many other parts of the dolphin's body may be involved in hearing. Some scientists think that dolphins may hear sounds through their lower jaws or from an area behind their pectoral fins. Other scientists suggest that the dolphins' blubber, the layer of fat under their skin, may also be involved in hearing.

We humans can see only with our eyes, but the dolphin has developed another sense, called *echolocation* or *sonar*, which enables it to "see" using sound that is reflected back from the dolphin's environment. The dolphin produces sequences of very short clicks that travel through the water and bounce off animals or other objects underwater. The reflected echoes of the clicks return to the dolphin and tell it what an object is made of, how big it is, and in which direction it is moving. Using echolocation, dolphins can find food and get other information about their environment that

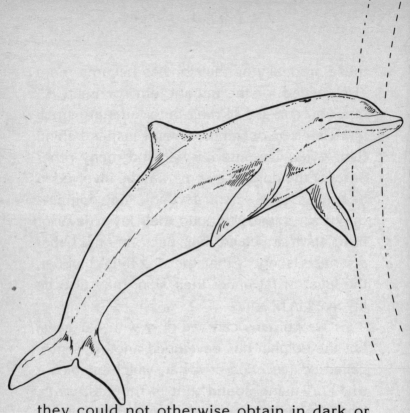

they could not otherwise obtain in dark or murky waters. They can tell the difference between different kinds of fish and avoid hidden fish hooks. Scientists have tested dolphins and discovered that they are able to tell the difference between small copper and steel disks the size of dimes. At oceanaria, dolphins have been taught to wear suction cups over their eyes as a "blindfold" and find and retrieve

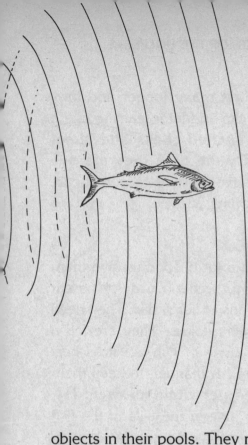

objects in their pools. They may also be able to tell if another dolphin in their group is pregnant by using their sonar to "see inside" it. We have often seen dolphins at Marine World scanning the bellies of pregnant dolphins.

When produced rapidly, their sonar clicks sometimes sound like a creaking door. If produced slowly, they sound like individual clicks. Young dolphins have to learn to echolocate. They first make longer and low-pitched types of clicks and later learn to make shorter and high-pitched clicks and direct them at objects. By the time they are two months old, they have learned to echolocate more like adult dolphins.

What Do Dolphins Eat?

Dolphins need a lot of food to give them energy. In oceanaria, bottlenose dolphins eat about 15 to 25 pounds of fish a day. They need more fish when it gets colder. They are fed a variety of different kinds of fish, such as herring, smelt, mackerel, and squid, to keep them healthy. They even get vitamins each day, which their trainers hide in the gills of the fish they eat. Dolphins in the wild may need even more fish and learn a lot of different ways of capturing fish, which we will discuss later.

The Playful Dolphin

Anyone who has watched dolphins at an oceanarium knows that they love to play. They play with each other, they play with people, and they play with all sorts of objects

Even dolphins take vitamins, which their trainers hide in the gills of the fish they eat.

such as balls, hoops, rings, floats, and Frisbees. Other things, such as leaves and feathers that blow into their pools, can also become toys. They seem to enjoy playing endless games of catch and tug-of-war with people. Some scientists have observed dolphins in the wild playing with seaweed, shells, fish, and other objects in the ocean.

Dolphins find all sorts of ways to play with things. Without the use of hands, they use the different parts of their bodies to manipulate their toys. For example, they often drag pieces of seaweed or leaves on their pectoral fins, their tail flukes, or their dorsal fins. Some dolphins use their whole bodies and glide on surfboards or other kinds of floats. They can even hold a surfboard under their bellies and swim in corkscrews through the water! A female dolphin at Marine World named Shilo once picked up a rock from the bottom of her pool by rolling on her back and sucking it onto her blowhole. She then proceeded to swim around the pool with it balanced on her head.

Delphi and Pan, our two young male dolphins at Marine World, love to play with volleyballs and rings, often playing with two or three of them at the same time. They invented a game in which one of them swims on the water surface upside down (on his back), holding a ring and a ball in his mouth. The dolphin tosses the ball up and down, catching it each time, without losing the ring in his mouth. Quite a feat! Another favorite game of theirs is dribbling a ball underwater, against the pool wall or the bottom of the tank. They invent all sorts of new games to play.

At Marine World we often found that the dolphins had wedged their toys, particularly their favorite balls, in crevices in their pool. We found these objects to be wedged in so tightly they were impossible for us to remove. But not so for the dolphins. They would easily free the toys and play with them and then wedge them back in the crevices again!

Bubble Rings

Dolphins love to play with objects that they are given or that they find. I have even seen them making their own toys! Several of the dolphins at Marine World Africa USA create beautiful rings made of air that they blow forcefully out of their blowhole. They look like shiny silver rings that rise slowly to the surface. The dolphins follow the "air rings" up to the water surface, often playing with them with their rostrums or tails. I have even seen a dolphin blow one ring, then a second ring that joined with the first to make a Hoola-Hoop-sized ring that the dolphin then swam through.

Sometimes other dolphins will watch as one dolphin blows bubble rings. One day, Shilo blew a series of bubble rings as three other dolphins watched. One of the other dolphins rapidly swam away and returned with a small piece of fish, which it placed in the rising ring. The piece

of fish spun around violently, caught in the turbulence of the rising ring of air. All the dolphins watched this with great interest, and they repeated the "experiment."

CHAPTER THREE

How Do Dolphins Communicate with Each Other?

One of the questions people always ask me is "How do dolphins communicate, and do they really have a language?" Some scientists used to think that because dolphins have such large brains and because they are such a social species, they might have their own language, as we do. Well, we might say that every animal that communicates with other members of its own group uses its own "language." Or, we might instead just say that the animals are using certain *signals* to communicate with each other.

We really are only beginning to learn about how dolphins communicate. We know that they use a variety of different sounds and behaviors when they interact with one another. Sometimes they are very quiet, and at other times they can be very vocal.

The noises they produce can be thought of as three different types of sounds: whistles, echolocation clicks, and a variety of other sounds like barks and squawks. We know that dolphins use echolocation for navigating through murky waters and seeing with sound. They may also use these echolocation clicks to communicate with one another.

It's not clear how dolphins make all of the different sounds they produce. We know that they make the whistles by moving air back and forth between air sacs, called nasal sacs, that are located inside of their heads below the blowhole. When they whistle, they don't usually release air from their blowholes, but once in a while you can see a stream of air bubbles escaping. This helps us identify who is whistling. Each dolphin uses many different kinds of whistles to communicate. We don't know what these different whistles mean or exactly how many different whistles they use, but at my laboratory we've counted over 60, and there are probably many more.

One really interesting thing scientists have discovered is that each dolphin has its

own particular whistle that it makes more than any other whistle. We call this a "signature whistle." One scientist developed a very small portable hydrophone (underwater microphone) that dolphins could actually wear while swimming around in their pools in an oceanarium. Using this hydrophone, the scientist was able to tell which dolphin was making whistles and which whistles it was using. He found that one female dolphin, Spray, would produce her signature whistle and also produce the signature whistle of her pool mate, Spotty. In the same way, Spotty most often produced his own signature whistle but also made Spray's whistle. The scientist thinks it is possible that when a dolphin makes another dolphin's signature whistle it might be calling the other dolphin or trying to get its attention, the way we use names.

As I watched Pan and Delphi grow up at Marine World, I learned a lot more about signature whistles. When they were first born, they made high-pitched squeals that sounded like a baby version of a whistle. Over the next few months, Delphi and Pan's own signature whistles began to sound a lot like their own mothers' signature whistles. We share our family names, and it will be interesting to learn if these animals do also.

Anyone who has visited an oceanarium is familiar with the loud squawks, chirps, and barks the dolphins also make. These sounds are the easiest ones for us to hear. During their play times, while they cavort and chase one another around the pool, they often squawk at one another, usually face-to-face

Dolphins make many different sounds.

with their mouths open. These squawks are sometimes used during friendly or playful times, but they can also be used as aggressive threats between dolphins.

We communicate like this also. We can use the same word in a variety of different situations, some playful, others angry. When we communicate, we listen to what others say, we look at the expressions on their faces and how their bodies look. Then we decide if people are angry or friendly and what they are really say-ing. It seems that dolphins and other animals may do something similar. Dolphins also use their bodies to communicate. They have all sorts of different postures and ways of holding their bodies in their three-dimensional world, where it is easy to swim upside down or hang vertically in the water with their heads down.

One friendly signal they make is showing their underside to another dolphin. We call this a *belly tilt* or *ventral presentation*. In the wild and in oceanaria, we have seen one dolphin approach another and show its belly, and then the two go off swimming together, sometimes caressing or rubbing each other on the way. Dolphins can also get the attention of other dolphins by swimming just in front of their heads.

We often see dolphins doing tail slaps on the water surface. This behavior can been both seen and heard, because their tails make a loud sound as they slap the water surface. This can sometimes be used as a warning signal or threat. At Marine World, our dolphins sometimes swim upside down past us and slap their tails on the surface. It looks like a combination of the friendly belly tilt and a tail slap. They may be using this kind of tail slap to get our attention.

Most people have seen dolphins *porpoise*. This is when they jump out of the water in graceful arches above the surface. At Marine World they often do this when they get excited, such as just before being fed. As soon as Delphi, Pan, Terry, and Circe spot us approaching their pools with buckets of fish, the water surface breaks with fast porpoising. When we first arrive at the lab in the morning, we are often greeted with porpoising, or the dolphins may breach. Breaching is when a dolphin leaps up out of the water and falls back down with its side or back hitting the water and causing a big splash. This also may be a signal they use to get the attention of others. And it does. Not only do you see them, but you also hear them as their bodies hit the water surface.

A porpoising dolphin.

There are many other sounds and behaviors the dolphins use among themselves. Perhaps we will soon understand more about their kind of communication. Wouldn't it be wonderful to really know what the different sounds and behaviors mean to dolphins?

All Animals Communicate

In order to survive in the wild, animals need to share information about one another and their environment. By using specific signals, animals can communicate with one another about their location, where food is, the presence of predators or other dangers, and their readiness to mate.

Animals use a variety of different kinds of signals to communicate. Some signals are visual and messages are sent by body posture, gestures, and movements. When a cat is defensive or afraid, it stands at its full height, with its back arched, its fur standing up (especially on its tail), its ears flat back, its mouth drawn back exposing its teeth, and its eyes open wide. Crabs and spiders communicate by waving their claws or legs in specific ways. Fiddler crabs wave their large claws when defending their burrows. Many species of fish communicate by changing color, and fireflies can communicate and find each other for mating by flashing pulses of light as night approaches.

Animals also use a wide variety of sounds to communicate. There are both vocal and nonvocal sounds. Different species have different vocal calls they use to share information. Wolves howl and have different howls for different situations. Birds sing and have different calls that they use in different situations. Scientists are finding that some species even have specific calls that they use to warn one another of different predators such as eagles, snakes, or leopards.

Some sounds are produced by animals doing certain behaviors. Gorillas and chimpanzees produce sounds by beating their chests. Dolphins produce nonvocal sounds by breaching and tail slapping.

Other species use vibrations, taste, touch, and smell to communicate. Many species release chemicals or odors to communicate with other members of their species. These signals are received by other individuals in the way of tastes or smells. Ants leave odor trails to inform other ants of a food source. Dogs and many other mammals urinate to claim their territory.

CHAPTER FOUR

Dolphin Societies

We know what it is to be a member of a society of people. Your society includes your friends and family, the people you go to school with and work with, and the rules you live by. Societies are important because they provide protection, food, and other important things. Above all, having a society makes it possible to cooperate with others and work together for everyone's good.

Dolphins live in large groups called *herds*, which are also societies. These societies of dolphins live in the oceans, bays, and rivers of the world. Bottlenose dolphins are found in the Atlantic, Pacific, Mediterranean, and Indian oceans. They inhabit both warm, tropical waters like those near Hawaii, the Galapagos Islands, the Gulf of Mexico, and the

Dolphins live in groups and depend on one another for survival.

Florida coast, and colder temperate waters like those off Scandinavia and the British Isles. They do not live in arctic regions, although several species of larger whales do.

Some species of dolphin live in the deeper waters of the oceans, miles off shore. These are called *pelagic* dolphins. Pacific bottlenose dolphins, for example, live in the eastern tropical Pacific Ocean and are often seen 1,000 miles off shore. Atlantic bottlenose dolphins, however, live closer to shore and spend much of their time in shallow waters just a few feet deep. They are the kind of dolphins most people are familiar with due to their popularity in oceanaria and on the television series "Flipper." They live off the coast of Florida, in the Gulf of Mexico, along the eastern coast of the United States, and in other Atlantic coastal regions. For this reason they are called *coastal dolphins.*

Whether coastal or pelagic, these "moving societies" of dolphins depend on one another for their survival. Living in the ocean is a lot different from living on land. Unlike humans and land animals, dolphins have no houses, caves, or shelters of any kind. The society itself is their only protection from predators and other threats in their environment. The size of these dolphin societies is quite variable. Some groups have up to 100 or even 1,000 dolphins, while other groups have only a few animals. It seems that dolphins that are pelagic, living in the deeper waters, live in larger groups than do coastal species. This may be because groups living in deeper waters need more members to work together and cooperate in catching fish, whereas groups that feed in shallower waters need fewer animals because they can use natural barriers such as the shoreline, sand bars, and reefs to help them trap fish.

These large societies in which the dolphins live are composed of smaller groups of dolphins called *subgroups*. The dolphins in these subgroups have long-lasting relationships and stay together for years. You can think of these as groups of close friends. It is important for individual dolphins to make a lot of friends. They work together and cooperate with one another to find and capture food.

They also protect each other from enemies, such as sharks or killer whales, and help and care for one another if they become injured, sick, or in danger. They give physical support to sick, injured, or very young animals by holding them at the water surface.

One or more dolphins do this by positioning their bodies below the injured dolphin and pushing it up to the surface. The supporting dolphins rise to the surface only to breathe, and they usually do not leave even to eat. They stop this behavior only when the sick dolphin either gets better or dies.

Another kind of help they give one another is called "standing by." This is when a dolphin stays with another dolphin who is in a dangerous situation. It's like staying with a friend who is in trouble or in danger. Rather than running away from a dangerous situation, we often choose to put ourselves in danger in order to help a friend.

Dolphins also "assist" one another. This is when one or more dolphins place themselves between a dolphin in danger and its enemies, thereby physically protecting their friend. For example, we often see dolphins trying to stop or block people who are trying to capture other dolphins.

This kind of behavior is called "altruism." In human society we think very highly of people who show this kind of behavior. We call

them heroes and heroines and give them medals of honor. In the situation of dolphins saving drowning humans, their behavior suggests that they may understand the dilemma of a drowning person and come to his or her rescue. This is altruism, too.

We see subgroups of dolphins both in the wild and in captivity. While dolphins develop and maintain their close friendships within their subgroups, they also mix and mingle with dolphins in other subgroups. This is like meeting with different groups of your friends. Most subgroups are made up of dolphins of either the same age or the same sex. For example, juveniles swim with other juveniles, and adults swim with adults. Groups of juvenile females and juvenile males also form their own groups.

The closest bonds are between mothers and their calves. Calves usually stay with their mothers for up to four to five years. Female calves tend to stay with their mothers longer than male calves do. Young males usually leave their mothers and form a group with other young males. Some scientists who have been watching bottlenose dolphins that live off the western Florida coast for 20 years have seen three generations of female dolphins living together in a subgroup made up of a grandmother, a mother, and a female calf.

Mothers with young calves form "nursery

The closest bonds in dolphin societies are between mother and calf.

groups" in which the youngsters are raised and protected. In these groups, dolphin mothers often work together to form a protective circle around their young calves, who then swim and play inside. There are even females that act as "aunts" and babysit, watching over the calves while their mothers are off feeding or doing other things.

53

Many bottlenose dolphins in the wild have "home ranges" in which they live. You can think about this like your neighborhood, the area in which you live, which may be several blocks or several miles in size. These dolphins live in specific areas that can range from a few miles to several hundred miles. Sometimes they venture out of their neighborhoods for a short time, but they come back to them. Other dolphins, like the bottlenose dolphins along the eastern coast of the United

States, migrate or move up and down the coastline.

Finding Food

Dolphins in the wild spend much of their day filling their stomachs. One of the most important things in the dolphin's life is finding fish. This affects why and when they go to different locations. Water temperature has a big effect on their lives, too, because fish follow certain water temperatures and dolphins follow the fish.

Dolphins have to be pretty flexible in their behavior because their environment is constantly changing. This means they have to be able to adapt or change what they do depending on the situation. They have to be able to search for fish, sometimes in new or unusual places. These smart creatures find all sorts of ways to get food. Sometimes they work in groups cooperatively as a team to herd a school of fish. The dolphins form a circle around the fish, and then individual dolphins rush into the circle and grab a fish.

Fish often follow tidal currents. Dolphins

can take advantage of this by positioning themselves facing into the current so that the fish are pushed to them. Fish also tend to be found in shallow areas along shorelines or near underwater reefs and sand bars. Dolphins use these natural barriers to trap fish.

Some dolphins follow fish into small rivers and chase them up onto the muddy banks. The dolphins actually slide out of the water and up onto the banks on their sides to grab the fish! Another method they use is to chase fish into shallow waters and then smack them with their tails to stun the fish.

Sometimes they discover a fishing boat trawling for shrimp. The fishermen throw overboard all the other kinds of fish they catch with the shrimp. One group of bottlenose dolphins in San Diego Bay in California learned to follow a boat that dumped garbage overboard. The garbage attracted all sorts of fish, and the dolphins followed along to eat the fish. What a variety of ways to get a meal!

Do you wonder what a day in the life of a dolphin is like? Well, we still have a lot to learn, but we think a typical day includes finding fish, traveling, playing, and in some cases mating. Many dolphins feed in the early morning and late afternoon. They spend the middle part of the day resting and playing together in groups, often at the water surface. Mating behavior often is seen at these times also. As we watch more social groups of dolphins in the wild, we hope to learn much more about their daily lives.

CHAPTER FIVE

A Dolphin
Is Born

At my laboratory at Marine World I've had the wonderful opportunity to observe several dolphin births. Terry and Circe, the two female bottlenose dolphins I work with and observe, gave birth to Pan and Delphi in 1983. I watched as the calves grew up and learned to communicate and interact with the other dolphins in their social group. Let me tell you about what I learned.

Female dolphins mature and can have babies at five to seven years old, while males tend to mature later, at 10-12 years old. Mother dolphins generally have only one calf at a time. They carry their unborn calf for 11 to 12 months before giving birth. This is called the *gestation* period. During this time, the calf develops to a point at which it can swim on its

Baby dolphins have to swim right after they are born.

own as soon as it is born. Baby dolphins are actually born with much more coordination and ability to interact in their environment than humans have right after birth. We are dependent on others to carry us around and feed us. But young dolphins have to swim right away and keep up with their mothers and the others in their group.

Infant dolphins are about three feet (90 centimeters) long and weight about 25 pounds (11 kilograms) when born. Their skin is a dark shade of gray that gradually turns lighter as they get older. At first, they take more frequent breaths than older dolphins do, often breathing four to six times a minute rather than two to three times a minute. But usually within the first week the infant gains more control over its breathing, and it rises to the water surface for a breath when its mother does.

It is not always easy to tell when an expectant mother is ready to give birth. By the 11th or 12th month, the mother's ventral side, or underside, has become much larger, and she looks much bigger than the other dolphins in her group. Sometimes when the mother dolphin is ready to give birth, she begins to move in different ways, arching and flexing her body backward and forward into a C-shaped curve. But this can begin several days before she actually gives birth. Sometimes she will refuse to eat fish, but this can also happen a few days before she actually gives birth.

One morning, Terry, our older female, refused to eat. She had been flexing her body for about a week. I grew very excited as I realized that she was about to give birth. I stayed at my laboratory all night, waiting. I had all my equipment ready: the video camera, tape recorder, hydrophone, and notebook. But there was no dolphin born that night. The next day, Terry seemed normal again, eating as usual and not flexing much. So I left for home. When I walked in my front door the telephone was ringing: Terry had begun to give birth! I was back at the lab in the wink of an eye.

The first clear sign of the birth is when the calf's tail flukes begin to emerge through

A baby dolphin emerges!

the mother's genital opening, called the genital slit. This opening is on the mother's underside just in front of her tail. Dolphins are usually born tail first, but some have been born head first. This is just the opposite of how we are born. Most human babies come out head first.

When I got to the lab, I could see the small, dark gray flukes sticking out a few inches from Terry's genital slit. As she swam in circles around the pool, she would often twist her body in corkscrew movements through the water. The calf's flukes moved in and then out a little more each time. Finally, after two hours, one half of the calf's body could be seen. Suddenly, Terry did another corkscrew and the calf was born. It immediately swam to the surface on its own and took its first breath.

Terry and the calf, the male we later named Pan, immediately swam together, bodies touching, the calf against his mother's side. The other dolphins in the pool were Circe, a younger pregnant female, and Gordo, the adult male who was the father. Both Circe and Gordo seemed very interested in the new

arrival. Circe started to swim with Terry and her new infant, while Gordo watched but kept his distance. Terry and Circe swam with the calf between them, protected in the middle. All night, I watched as they continued to swim in this way. Sometimes Pan would make sounds that were like baby versions of adult whistles. They sounded more like little squeal-whistles. Terry would also whistle her signature whistle, but it was generally very quiet that first night.

Two days later, Circe refused to eat. She had been flexing for several days. This time I was determined to stay until the dolphin gave birth. At 6:00 P.M., as it began to grow dark, I saw small gray flukes begin to emerge from her genital slit. By 8:00 that evening, Delphi was born! Like Pan, he also swam to the surface on his own and took his first breath. But Circe did not go to Delphi. Instead she swam around the pool alone. I watched and listened to see what would happen. The dolphins were very quiet. Circe swam three times around the pool without approaching her little calf. He was bobbing alone at the surface. Suddenly, there was a long and complicated whistle, and Circe immediately swam to Delphi and they began to swim together just as Terry and Pan had done. Everything was just fine after that.

Who made the whistle? Did it tell Circe what to do? Later, I analyzed the tapes I had recorded of the births. I used special equipment that shows me "sonagrams," which means sound pictures of the dolphins' whistles or other vocalizations. It looked like the whistle that we heard just before Circe approached Delphi had Terry's signature at the end of it. I think that it was Terry whistling and that perhaps she was "telling" Circe what to do. But we need to do more studies before we know for sure.

Circe and Delphi swim together.

As we discussed earlier, dolphin calves nurse from their mothers. Usually, newborn dolphins begin to nurse within 12 hours after they are born. The calves have to find their mother's teats, which are located on the underside of her body on both sides of the genital slit inside two smaller slits.

A calf nurses, its tongue forming a watertight seal around the mother's teat.

(Remember, dolphins have become very streamlined for their aquatic life and everything is inside their sleek bodies.) Calves actually curl their tongues around the mother's teat, forming a waterproof seal so no milk escapes and no water gets in. As the calf sucks, milk is squirted into its mouth.

Newborn dolphins don't have to learn to suck or nurse from their mothers. It is an automatic response. But they do have to learn where to nurse from. Sometimes, calves have trouble at first figuring out where to nurse. The mothers help by turning their undersides to the infant until the infant practically bumps into the right place. Once the calves begin to nurse they learn where to go quickly.

A calf bumps into its mother. Sometimes baby dolphins have trouble figuring out where to nurse.

Infant dolphins are not born with much blubber, the layer of fat that keeps these mammals warm in the water. Newborn dolphins have to get a lot of their mothers' rich milk so they can build up a layer of blubber. Milk also gives them the energy they need. They usually nurse about every 15 to 30 minutes during the first weeks, but they nurse only for several seconds at a time. Within a few days, they look fatter and more rounded out.

From the very first hours after birth, mothers and calves use whistles we call contact calls if they are separated from each other. Lots of other mammals use contact calls in similar ways. During these early days the young dolphins are learning about their world and the rules of their society. In the next chapter we'll talk about growing up as a dolphin.

CHAPTER SIX

Growing Up

Dolphin societies are complex, and there are a lot of rules to learn. Like young children, calves learn new things every day. At my laboratory I watched as Pan and Delphi learned how to behave from their mothers. During the first few days after their births, Terry and Circe, the mother dolphins, usually kept their calves right next to them throughout the day and night. Before Pan and Delphi were born, the mothers would usually stop swimming and rest while lying at the water surface, but after the births, the mothers continually circled around the pool without stopping to rest. After a few days they gradually began to slow down, occasionally stopping for short periods. At these times, their calves would circle them, staying close by. They had already learned to

Newborn dolphins stay very close to their mothers.

stay with their mothers. But sometimes they would depart from their mothers, rushing across the pool. Terry and Circe would race after them, whistling until they were reunited. Then all grew quiet again.

The two mothers and their calves formed a group and usually swam together. Gordo, the father, usually swam or rested apart from the group, but on occasion he joined in for a swim.

If Delphi or Pan continued to depart repeatedly from their mothers, more drastic steps were taken. The mother would push her calf to the bottom of the pool and hold him there for several seconds. When released, the calf would usually behave himself and stay with his mother. This kind of reprimand has been seen in most oceanaria that have had dolphin births. As the young dolphins grow larger, it is harder for their mothers to hold them down like this. So, instead, their mothers go underneath them and hold them above the water surface. But Delphi and Pan were just like other young dolphins that have been

observed in oceanaria, and they quickly returned to their mothers' sides when they were tired or alarmed. When they were together, it was usually quiet.

With each day, it seemed that Terry and Circe allowed Pan and Delphi to leave them for longer periods of time. The two calves began to approach each other and play together. We gave them all sorts of objects to play with such as balls, rings, floats, and inner tubes. When they were just a few weeks old they had already invented all sorts of ways to play with their toys. Usually their mothers would watch them from a distance as they played, finally calling them back with a whistle or an approach.

Delphi and Pan began to approach their father, too, often swimming quickly toward him and then passing back and forth in front of his head. Gordo was a big, friendly dolphin and was always gentle with the young dolphins.

Sometimes one of the mothers would take care of both calves while the other mother rested alone. The mothers would take turns playing "aunt." This behavior is another way in which dolphins help each other and cooperate within their society.

Like us, dolphins learn a lot of things by observing others and imitating what they see. Young dolphins stay with their mothers for a long time. Learning by observing and interacting with their mothers and other members of their social group is extremely important.

During their first six months of life, Delphi and Pan were nursing, and they only watched as we fed their mothers fish. They began to nurse less often, once every hour or two, but they were growing rapidly. Then the young dolphins began to "mouth" and play with the herring and smelt their mothers were fed or that we offered them. Sometimes it looked like their mothers were intentionally dropping fish near them, because Terry and Circe rarely let a fish escape their mouths under normal conditions. At the end of the day, a diver had to go into their pool and remove all of the fish the young males had played with and partially chewed.

By their 10th month, Pan and Delphi

A diver removed these partially chewed fish from the dolphins' pool after Delphi and Pan practiced their new eating skills.

began to actually eat fish, but they still continued to nurse from their mothers. We used to think that dolphins were weaned (stopped nursing) by the time they were one or one-and-one-half years old. But by watching Delphi and Pan, and observing other dolphins in the wild, we now think they often continue nursing for up to four years if their mother does not give birth to another calf during this period of time. Some scientists have even observed a seven-year-old male still nursing from his mother in the wild. In the wild, young dolphins stay with their mothers in their subgroups and probably observe how they capture fish. We don't know too much yet about this process, but we think that the youngsters eventually try it themselves, imitating what the others do. They learn to work as a team with the other dolphins in their group.

Gordo watches Delphi and Pan eat.

Learning by Observing

The fact that dolphins learn by imitation and observation is clear to anyone who has worked with these incredible mammals. Dolphins can watch other dolphins being taught a certain behavior by a trainer and then do it themselves. They often imitate what they see. At one oceanarium, a dolphin who performed a series of behaviors in a dolphin show refused to perform one day. One of his pool mates quickly took his place and did all of his behaviors perfectly. The stand-in had never been taught to do this: She had learned through observation.

I observed an interesting case of rapid learning by observation. We never saw Delphi and Pan—who were living in a separate pool from the dolphins that produced bubble rings—blow bubble rings. One day, I gave Pan a hand signal to fetch a fish that was on the bottom of the pool. He immediately dove down and picked up the fish. I

praised him loudly as he began to pick up the fish, but he dropped it on the way back up to the surface. As he dropped it, he released a burst of air, as often occurs when dolphins are frustrated or surprised. The burst of air formed a bubble ring, and I quickly pointed to it and praised Pan. He dashed down to the bottom of the pool again, positioned himself near the dropped fish, and blew another bubble ring. I made a specific signal with my arm as he made the bubble ring and praised him again. When he returned to the surface, I gave him the new signal again, and he immediately swam down to the pool bottom and produced a third bubble ring. A case of quick learning! Then Delphi and Pan together positioned in front of me. I gave the new signal once more, and both dolphins swam down to the bottom of the pool and made bubble rings! It seemed that Delphi had learned to do this just by observing and imitating Pan.

Dolphins imitate a lot of things that they see and hear. We think they learn to communicate by imitating the whistles and other sounds their mothers and other group members use, just as we learn our own language.

There are many stories about how dolphins have imitated behaviors that they have seen people or other animals do. For example, one dolphin living in an oceanarium in South Africa watched a diver who was cleaning the pool. The diver was cleaning algae off of the sides of the walls and the pool floor with a scraper. He wore a scuba tank so he could breathe underwater, and the exhaust from his scuba gear released air bubbles, which rose to the water surface. After watching for a while, the dolphin found a piece of broken tile on the pool floor and began to use it to scrape off the algae from its pool just like the diver! He even released streams of air bubbles from his blowhole as he did this!

Another young dolphin at the same oceanarium was looking at people standing next to an underwater observation window. We usually think that underwater windows are

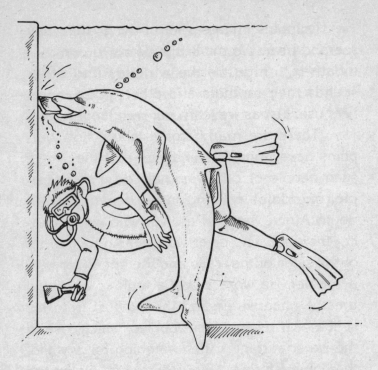

designed so *we* can watch the *dolphins*, but they watch us, too. This young dolphin watched several people as they stood by the window. They were talking among themselves and not paying much attention to the dolphin. One woman was smoking a cigarette, and she released a big billow of smoke in front of the dolphin's window. The young dolphin raced over to its mother and appeared to nurse for a second or so. Then, he raced back to the same window where the people were and released a large, billowing cloud of milk right in front of the window! That certainly got their attention, as well as the attention of the director of the oceanarium.

This same director told of another dolphin that shared its pool with a seal. Seals and dolphins swim in very different ways. The dol-

phin began to imitate the way the seal swam and then tried to mate with the seal.

I have watched Delphi and Pan imitate each other and even the way objects move. Sometimes one of the young dolphins will invent a new game with his toys and then the other dolphin will do the same thing. For example, Delphi began to carry three balls in his mouth at the same time, and then Pan began to do the same thing. One day I saw Pan playing with his "fish float" in an interesting way. The fish float is a two-foot-long toy fish made out of heavy white rubber. It is filled with air and floats on the water surface. The dolphins frequently dragged the fish float along the water surface in their mouths. But this day, Pan carried the fish float to the very bottom of the pool and then released it from his mouth. As the fish float rose to the surface, it zigzagged upward. Pan followed it up and zigzagged also, imitating its behavior. It was a new game! He took the fish float down to the bottom of the pool over and over again, zigzagging his way up with the float as it rose. Later in the day, I saw Delphi do the same thing.

So it seems we have a lot in common with dolphins, even though we are very different from each other and come from really different environments. We both learn a lot of things by watching, listening, and imitating.

CHAPTER SEVEN

How Smart Are Dolphins?

Another question people always seem to ask is "How intelligent are dolphins, and are they as smart as we are?" And I tell them that it's hard to know how smart other animals are because we usually compare them to ourselves. Animals may have a very different kind of intelligence than humans, and their intelligence may not be evident when we try to judge it by human standards.

What does it mean to be intelligent? We all think we can recognize intelligence, but it's not so easy to define it. Perhaps we can think of intelligent behavior as coming up with solutions to problems in lots of different and changing situations. For example, if you wanted to reach a breakable cookie jar that was high up on a shelf way out of your reach,

Dolphins' intelligence may be very different from ours.

would you: (1) jump up and down and try to reach it, (2) ask your little brother or sister to get it, (3) find a chair that you could climb on to reach it, or (4) ask your mother or father to get it for you five minutes before dinner time? You would have to figure out which solution would get you the cookies.

You might make a different choice if you had wings and could fly. Because they live in a different environment and have different bodies, dolphins make different choices and find different solutions also. So, when we try to understand dolphin intelligence we have to consider the world in which they live and what's important to them.

Unlike us, the nonhanded dolphins don't build houses, paint pictures, or write books. But they have survived for millions of years and have complex societies. Although they are an intelligent species, their kind of intelligence may be very different from ours.

We have already talked about some of the ways in which dolphins show intelligence, such as when they imitate the behavior of others or learn from and help one another. I have seen other things that dolphins do that also suggest their kind of intelligence. It can be difficult to design specific experiments that show how intelligent other animals are, but long and careful observations of their behavior can give us a better idea of how their minds may work.

Let's look at one such story that occurred at Marine World. The head dolphin trainer, Jim Mullen, has worked closely with dolphins for many years and often works with them as a team. He taught the dolphins to bring him pieces of paper or leaves that blew into their pool. He rewarded them with a fish

every time they brought him back something. One day, one of the older male dolphins, named Spock, began bringing Jim back small pieces of brown paper, like that from a brown paper bag. Spock brought back one small piece of brown paper after another, each time getting a fish from Jim. Jim began to grow suspicious, and he went to get a better look through an underwater window. A brown paper bag was wedged in a crevice under a platform, and Spock was ripping off small pieces of it and trading them in for fish rewards! No one knew if Spock had wedged the bag in the crevice on purpose so he could trade in one piece at a time in order to get more fish, or if the bag just got stuck and he took advantage of the situation. But his behavior certainly suggests intelligence.

Another example took place at an oceanarium in Hawaii. One day, a dolphin who had been performing a set of behaviors in a certain order for years refused to do the correct behaviors during a dolphin show. Usually, the trainer would give the dolphin a specific hand signal, the dolphin would do the correct behavior, and the trainer would reward the dolphin with a fish. But this time when the trainer gave her a signal to do a leap she did a different behavior. She kept doing all the wrong behaviors during the show. This puzzled her trainer because this dolphin had been performing the same sequence for years and knew it well. What could be going on? Can you guess? The trainer finally realized that the fish he was giving the dolphin was spoiled and this was the dolphin's way of letting him know something was wrong.

It is really fascinating to watch dolphins and let them show us how smart they are. In the next chapter, you will read about some of the experiments that other scientists and I have done to learn more about their intelligence and communication.

CHAPTER EIGHT

Communicating with Dolphins

The author and one of the dolphins of Project Circe.

The word communicate means "to share." When we communicate, we share our ideas and thoughts with others. We can tell others how we feel and find out what they are thinking and feeling. We can talk about the things and people around us and how we feel about them.

Wouldn't it be exciting to be able to communicate with another species, such as the dolphin? Some people think that only humans are able to communicate, but scientists who study animal communication and behavior are finding out that all animals communicate among themselves. Insects, fish, birds, reptiles, and mammals all communicate in different ways using different kinds of signals. We've talked about the fact that dolphins use sounds and different postures and body movements to communicate with one another. We humans use our own kinds of sounds and our bodies to communicate with other humans. When we work or interact with dolphins, many kinds of informal communication begin.

For example, at my laboratory, if I am standing at the side of the dolphin pool and

Circe gets a rub.

Circe swims over to me and rolls onto her side, I usually begin to rub her. She really seems to enjoy this and will usually stay with me. So, when I see Circe roll toward me like this, it communicates to me that she wants a rub, and she probably continues to do this because it gets her a rub. If I come out early in

92

the morning before the dolphins have eaten their first meal of fish, Circe often comes over to me with a big open mouth. This does not mean "rub me" but, rather, "feed me."

Eye contact is very important when you interact with dolphins. It lets you both know that you are doing something together. The dolphins will often swim past you and look at you while they do a particular behavior. Their eye contact lets you know the behavior is directed at you.

Eye contact is an important part of communication.

You quickly learn what many of their actions mean, or at least what you should do in response to them. At the same time, the dolphins are also learning what our actions mean, or what they should do. If I put my arm in the water and move it from side to side, that lets the dolphins know that I want to rub them. The signal that I use to ask them to come over for a rub is different from their signal to me. This kind of communication is very informal and develops as our relationship with each other grows deeper. When we learn to communicate we test what happens when we do certain things. How do others around us react? Does what you do get the reaction that you wanted? If so, you probably try it again. If it works again then you might begin to use it to communicate.

Let me give you another example of how communication can develop. Several years ago, when I was a graduate student, I was working with another young dolphin, also named Circe. I was in charge of feeding her three times a day. I would prepare her fish by cutting it into three sections, the head, middle,

and tail. I quickly learned that she would gladly eat the heads and middles but would refuse to eat the tail sections. So I experimented and finally realized that she would eat the tails if I cut off the fins. Circe had taught me how she liked her fish.

If I wanted to let Circe know that she did something wrong I would just back away from the poolside for a minute or so and look at her. This is called a "time out," and it is often

used by dolphins trainers for the same purpose. When this happened, Circe would just
watch me and wait for me to return to her, and
then she would usually do the correct thing.
Then one day, I accidently gave her a tail sec-
tion of fish without the fins cut off. She immediately dropped the fish and swam away from
me and went to the other side of the pool and
just looked at me. After a few seconds, I got
the strong feeling that she was giving *me* a

time out! Being a scientist, I decided to try this again several days later and see what she would do. Sure enough, every time I gave her an uncut tail, she would give me a "time out." In this case, we both learned to use the same signal to communicate.

These are informal yet interesting ways in which we can learn to communicate with dolphins. But there are also more formal scientific experiments that have been going on to see how much dolphins can really understand when we teach them artificial languages or communication codes.

At the University of Hawaii, Dr. Louis Herman and his colleagues have taught two Atlantic bottlenose dolphins, Phoenix and Akeakami, to understand different gestures, "gestural sentences," or sequences of sounds. The researchers give the dolphins a particular hand signal or set of gestures and teach the dolphins to do certain behaviors in response. If the dolphins perform the correct behavior, they get a fish reward. For example, by giving the dolphins different combinations of gestures, the researchers can ask the dolphins to do different things, such as "fetch ball," "fetch ring," "jump over hoop," or "flipper touch ring." The dolphins have to watch and understand all the gestures in a sequence in order to know what behavior to do and what object to do it with. This is different from what you usually see in dolphin shows in oceanaria in which the dolphins are given one gesture that means "fetch the ball" and another signal that means "fetch the hoop." The dolphins have shown us that they can learn to understand these signals and can often immediately figure out new combinations of hand signals that they are given.

In my research program with Delphi, Pan, Terry, and Circe, we have taken a different approach. I decided that rather than asking the dolphins to respond to our requests, we should give them the chance to ask us for things. To do this, I designed an underwater keyboard for the dolphins. They use this keyboard to ask for things they want, such as toy balls, rings, hoops, floats, disks, or rubs. The keyboard has nine different keys that display different-shaped forms. When a dolphin push-

The author designed this keyboard to let the dolphins in Project Circe ask for the things they want.

es one of the forms, a computer-generated whistle is played, and the dolphin gets a particular object or activity.

For example, if Delphi pushes the key showing the triangle, a particular whistle is played to him in the pool, and he is given a ball. If he pushes the key with the H shape, he hears a different whistle, and he is given a rub.

The computer whistles that the dolphins hear each time they push a key sound like dolphin whistles, but they are actually different from any of the whistles that our dolphins use normally. We were really surprised, then, when we began to hear the dolphins imitate the computer whistles. Pan and Delphi started to produce copies of the computer-generated whistles after hearing them only a few times. They sometimes made these whistles before they pushed the key that would make the same whistle. Other times, they would make the whistle that was associated with the toy with which they were playing. For example, Delphi sometimes whistled the ball whistle while he was playing with a toy ball. He didn't whistle it when he was playing with toy rings.

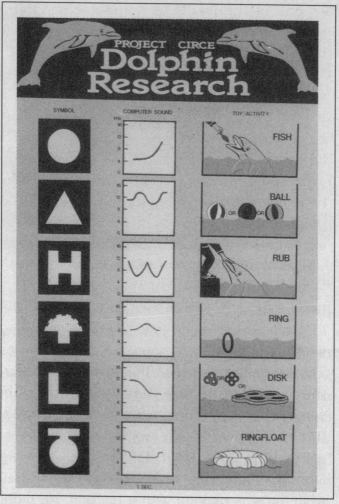

This chart explains the different symbols on the keyboard.

Two dolphins push keys on the keyboard as the author watches.

Instead, he would produce the ring whistle.

This experiment told us a lot about how dolphins learn. It made it even clearer to us that dolphins learn a lot by imitation. It also suggested that dolphins may have their own sounds that they use to refer to things in their world. As we work with and watch these intelligent mammals, we learn more and more about their abilities.

Top: *A dolphin gets a rub.*
Bottom: *A dolphin gets a ring.*

Dolphins on Duty

The U.S. Navy has been studying the capabilities of dolphins for many years. Many people in the navy feel that dolphins would make excellent helpers to underwater divers. It has been suggested that they could carry tools down to divers and assist them in many ways. The navy has trained dolphins to detect underwater mines and other targets by using their vision and echolocation. Dolphins and pilot whales have been trained to do open ocean work in which they follow a navy boat out into the ocean and perform specific underwater tasks, such as retrieving sunken objects. The animals are trained to wear a special harness on their heads that can pick up objects from the ocean floor. This type of open ocean work requires a great deal of training because the animals could decide to swim away.

Recently, there have been several newspaper stories about the navy training dolphins to protect

United States nuclear submarine facilities off the coast of Seattle, Washington. There has been a widespread public protest against the use of dolphins for this purpose. Many environmentalists and animal welfare groups are worried that the waters off Seattle are too cold for dolphins, and others feel they should not be enlisted for defense activities.

How do you feel about using dolphins for defensive purposes? Try to discuss this with your class and see how others feel about this issue.

Most dolphins live in the wild, and it is crucial to preserve their natural environment.

CHAPTER NINE

Protecting Dolphins: What You Can Do

In this book, I've talked about the dolphins' world—their watery home—and the way they live in it within their societies. By observing them in an oceanarium, I have found out a lot about their communication and behavior. However, most dolphins live in the wild, and it is crucial to preserve their natural environment. People who work with dolphins hope that the more understanding we have of the dolphins and their world, the more we will respect them and want to protect them.

When we learn about the dolphins' home we are learning about their "ecology." The word *ecology* comes from the Greek word for house. We know that dolphins don't have houses like we do. Instead, their whole environment—the water around them and the other species they share it with—is their home. Just as our houses protect us, the dolphins have to have good "houses" for protection. If their environment is in danger, so are the dolphins.

We've all heard terrible stories in the news about how our seas are becoming polluted. We hear about oil spills and toxic chemical and hospital waste being dumped into our waters. We see heartbreaking photographs of marine mammals and sea birds lying dead on the beach after having been caught in a drift net or fishing line or having swallowed a plastic bag someone left on the beach. These things destroy the dolphins' world and threaten their lives.

Pollution

For the past few years, hundreds of dolphins living off the East Coast of the United States and in the Mediterranean sea have died from a mysterious virus. Many marine mammal specialists think that this happened because of pollutants that have been dumped in their environment.

Dolphins need fish to survive. The fish they eat survive in turn by eating aquatic plants and microorganisms. This is what we call the food chain, who eats whom. What do you think happens when toxic chemicals and waste are dumped into the oceans? The plants and microorganisms take in water and hold concentrations of these pollutants. Then fish eat the plants and microorganisms, and the pollutants get passed on to them. Then the dolphins eat the fish and get sick.

Unlike us, when dolphins get sick they can't stay home and get into bed and give their bodies a chance to get better. They have to keep swimming, which requires a lot of energy. A sick dolphin usually doesn't want to eat or can't eat, so it doesn't get the energy it needs to survive. Many scientists think that once a dolphin gets sick and weak because of polluted fish, it is more vulnerable to other viruses in its environment. This may be what happened to all the dolphins that died on the East Coast.

What can you do to help? There are environmental groups that work hard to protect our waters. Get involved and support their efforts. Talk to your parents, schoolmates, and other friends about the problem. Call or visit the offices of the environmental groups in your area that are working on this problem and ask how you can help. Maybe they can send your class materials on what you can do, and you can turn it into a special class project.

Our government is in charge of regulating what gets dumped into our waters. The environmental groups can tell you the names of the people in your local government and in Washington, D.C., who you can write to about your concerns. Don't think that a letter from you or a letter from your whole class doesn't have an effect. Try it. If enough people write in, it can make a difference.

Another thing you can do is to be sure that when you are at the beach, you clean up before you leave. Take all the paper and plastic things with you and throw them away in a covered can or take them home and dispose of them. Even a small plastic toy ball can kill a marine mammal if it is swallowed. Six-packs of soda or other beverages usually are held together with plastic rings. Birds and marine mammals often get stuck in these rings or get them twisted around their necks. You can avoid this problem by cutting the rings into pieces before you throw them away. If this will

not be possible, don't bring them to the beach at all. Look around you. Have others left a mess? Clean it up! Maybe you can organize a day with your friends to clean up one of your local beaches. It really feels great to know that you are helping. It also gives other people the same idea.

Fishing Nets

Another big problem for dolphins and other marine mammals are drift nets. Many fishermen off the Pacific and Atlantic coasts and in other countries all over the world use large drift nets to catch fish. Miles of these fishing nets are placed in the water so that the fishermen can intercept schools of fish travelling through the waters and haul up large catches. But these nets catch a lot more than just fish. The nets are hard to see and stretch for miles so it's hard to avoid them. Marine mammals such as whales, dolphins, seals, sea lions, and otters get tangled up and caught in the nets. They are unable to come to the water surface to breathe and they die. Sometimes even if they can get to the surface, they are so

This tragic photo shows a dolphin caught in a fishing net.

badly tangled that they cannot escape. They are unable to eat and they die.

Many environmental groups are working to ban the use of these deadly nets. Get involved. Again, call your local environmental group and see how you can help. Get materials from them. Read about the problem in the newspaper and talk to your teacher and class about it.

Holding up a portion of a three-mile-long drift net, kids join in a protest against the use of the fishing device.

What you do can really help. For example, you have probably heard about the dolphin-tuna situation. Tuna fishermen who fish for tuna in the eastern tropical Pacific and in Mediterranean waters use purse seine nets to catch yellowfin tuna. For some reason, dolphins and tuna swim together in these areas.

The fishermen drop their nets around the dolphins and tuna, trapping them inside. The top of the net is then closed like a purse. The dolphins get tangled in the nets and many die, either because they are unable to breathe or are injured in the process of the nets' being hauled onto the tuna boats. Environmental groups were able to get video footage showing this terrible and inhumane situation and took it to the news media. People were shocked.

Many people got involved in trying to stop the tuna industry from this practice. Thousands of students and their classes wrote to the government asking them to stop this situation. Schools across the country stopped serving tuna in their lunchrooms after students petitioned their school boards. Many of the big tuna companies now show advertisements saying that they will not buy tuna that is caught in this way. So some progress has been made. But tuna fishermen are still using these nets, and dolphins are still being caught with the tuna. These fishermen continue to sell the tuna to other companies in the United States and elsewhere in the world.

So if you do eat tuna, make sure you buy it only in cans that are marked "Dolphin Safe." If your store doesn't have it, ask the management if they can get it and explain why.

In this book, I've shared some of what I've learned about dolphins, from my own work with them and that of others. Above all, I've tried to tell you about what they have shown us of their world. Their survival is dependent on team work and helping one another. Let's take a cue from them and try to work together as a team to protect them and their environment, their home. It's our home, too.

GLOSSARY

Assisting: When one or more dolphins place themselves between a dolphin in danger and its enemy.

Aunting: When a female dolphin watches over calves while their mothers are away.

Belly tilt: A friendly signal made when one dolphin shows its underside to another dolphin. Also called a *ventral presentation*.

Blowhole: Two openings that are the dolphin's nostrils on the top of its head.

Breaching: When a dolphin leaps up out of the water and falls back down with its side or back hitting the water and causing a big splash.

Calf: A young dolphin.

Coastal dolphins: Dolphin species that live close to shore.

Contact call: A whistle used by mothers and calves in the first few hours after birth in case they become separated.

Dorsal region: The dolphin's upper body.

Echolocation: A sense that helps the dolphin "see" through dark or murky water using sound as it is reflected back from the dolphin's environment.

Flukes: The large, flat horizontal fins at the end of a dolphin's tail.

Herd: A large group of dolphins that lives and travels together.

Oceanarium: An aquarium for marine mammals.

Orca: Killer whale.

Pectoral fins: Dolphins' flippers.

THE SECRETS OF THE DOLPHINS

Pelagic dolphins: Dolphin species that live in the deeper waters of the oceans.

Photoidentification: A method of telling dolphins apart by looking at photographs of them and comparing their dorsal fins.

Porpoising: When a dolphin jumps out of the water in graceful arches above the surface.

Rostrum: The dolphin's beak.

Signature whistle: The whistle that a particular dolphin makes more than any other whistle.

Standing by: When a dolphin stays with another dolphin who is in a dangerous situation.

Subgroup: A smaller group of dolphins within a herd. Dolphins in subgroups look for food together and help and protect one another.

Time out: When a dolphin trainer backs away from poolside and looks at the dolphin. This lets the dolphin know that it has done something wrong.

Ventral region: The dolphin's belly.

Vibrissae: Little hairs on baby dolphins' beaks that fall out a few days after birth.

INDEX

ABOUT THE CONTRIBUTORS:

DIANA REISS was born in Philadelphia, Pennsylvania, and earned her Ph.D. in speech and communication science from Temple University. On a grant from the French Ministry of Culture, she studied bio-acoustics for two years at the Laboratory of Physiological Acoustics, National Center for Zoological Research (C.N.R.Z.) in France. Since 1981, she has been research director of Project Circe, a study of dolphin communication, cognition, and behavior at Marine World Africa U.S.A. in Vallejo, California. She is also on the faculty of San Francisco State University, where she teaches courses on human and animal communication.

LAURIE O'KEEFE is a freelance illustrator who lives with her menagerie—ferrets, chinchillas, rabbits, an English bulldog, a Samoyed, and a Patagonian conure—in the mountains of Colorado.

Author's acknowledgments: To my husband, Dr. Stuart Firestein, and to Dr. Rene-Guy Busnel, Marine World Foundation, and the wonderful staff of Project Circe. I especially thank Circe, Terry, Delphi, and Pan for their inspiration.